Roses and Flowering Branches
in Counted Cross Stitch

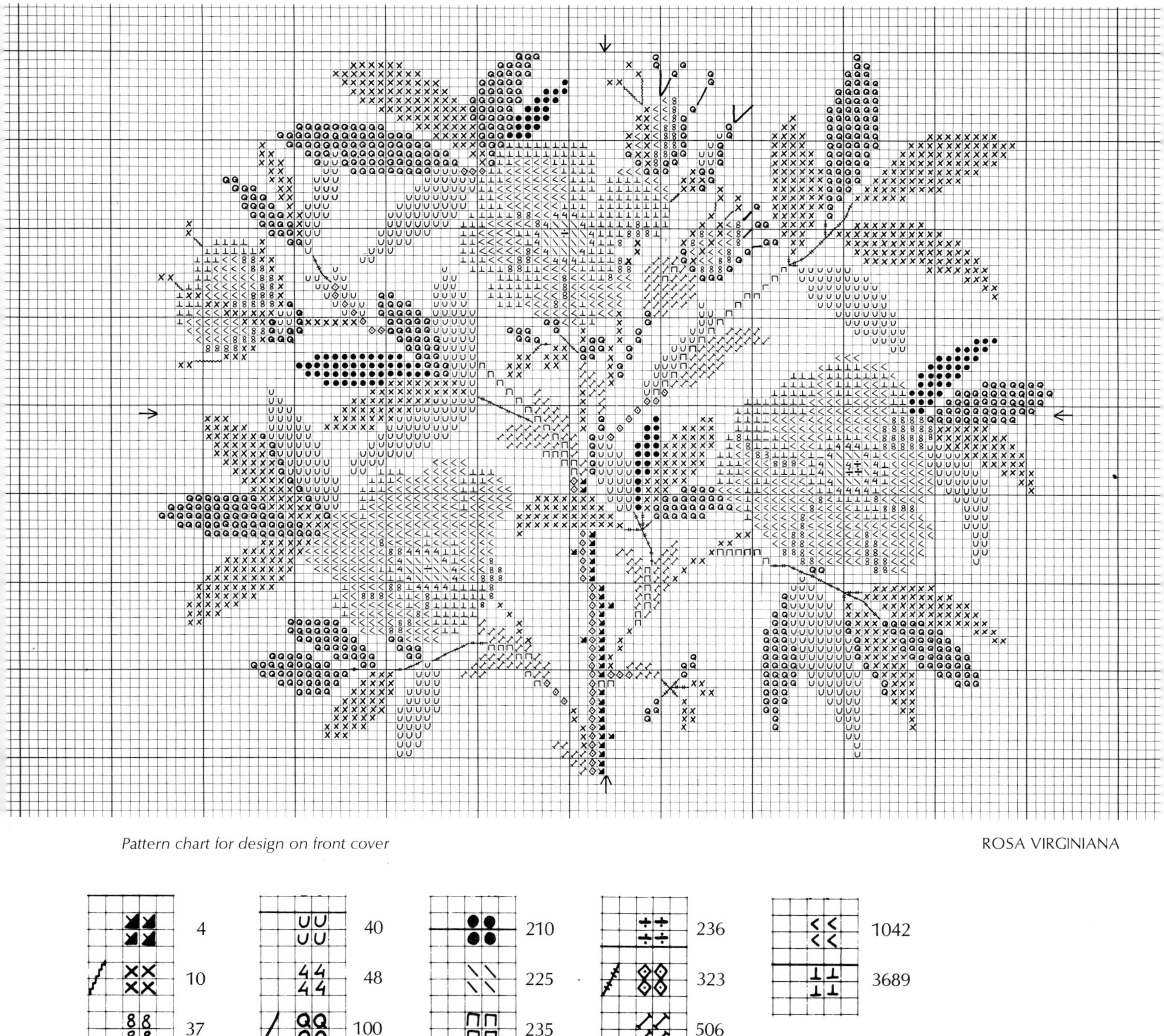

Pattern chart for design on front cover

ROSA VIRGINIANA

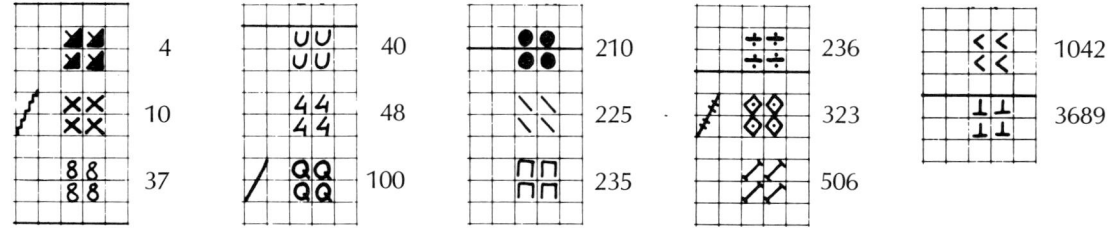

	4
	10
	37
	40
	48
	100
	210
	225
	235
	236
	323
	506
	1042
	3689

Roses and Flowering Branches in Counted Cross Stitch

by Gerda Bengtsson
from the Danish Handcraft Guild

Prentice Hall Press · New York

Contents

Copyright © 1985, 1986 by Selskabet til Haandarbejdets Fremme and Høst & Søns Forlag. All rights reserved, including the right of reproduction in whole or in part in any form.

Published in 1986 by Prentice Hall Press
A Division of Simon & Schuster, Inc.
Gulf + Western Building
One Gulf + Western Plaza
New York, NY 10023

Originally published in Denmark by Høst & Søns Forlag, Copenhagen in 1986 under the title Roser og blomstrende grene i korssting

Published in Great Britain in 1986 by Bell & Hyman Publishers under the title Flowers and Berries in Cross Stitch

PRENTICE HALL PRESS is a trademark of Simon & Schuster, Inc.

Library of Congress Cataloging-in-Publication Data

Bengtsson, Gerda.
　Roses and flowering branches in counted cross-stitch.

　1. Cross-Stitch-Patterns. 2. Decoration and ornament-Plant forms. I. Title.
TT771.B3624　1986　746.44　86-9450
ISBN 0-13-783291-5

Printed in Denmark

10 9 8 7 6 5 4 3 2 1

First Prentice Hall Press Edition

Pattern for the front-cover piece　2

Materials and instructions　7

Method of working　8

Color chart　9

Examples of finished work　10

Patterns　13-63

List of patterns　64

Suppliers　64

Preface

Each year The Danish Handcraft Guild publishes a calendar of cross stitch designs. This book combines the flower designs from two such calendars.

The roses and berries in this book are designed by Gerda Bengtsson who is Denmark's most popular flower illustrator. She has worked extensively for the Danish Handcraft Guild and her reputation has spread to many parts of the world through her cross stitch designs.

Few people are as familiar with the Danish flora as Gerda Bengtsson. She is a flower connoisseur. When she observes flowers she always does so with a view to drawing them. She is aware that her roses and berries must not only be lifelike, but also have to be designed to make beautiful, artistic compositions.

In order to avoid large areas of single color Gerda Bengtsson prefers plants with small flowers and berries. Rather than cultivated garden roses with their large, single-colored petals, she therefore seeks out wild roses with hip berries. Most of the roses and berries are predominantly red, but yellow and white are included to contrast sensitively with the brown branches and green leaves. The browns and greens also vary subtly in shading, from light to dark, demonstrating Gerda Bengtsson's fine sense of color.

The designs are worked in a wide range of Danish Flower Threads, but they also include light cross stitch thread and silk to provide gloss and brightness.

The author uses flowers from her own garden and those of her friends. N.G. Treschow, from the Botanical Gardens in Copenhagen, helps her by providing fresh flowers out of season and he also assists with the identification of the roses and berries.

Eric Lassen, President of The Danish Handcraft Guild

The Danish Handcraft Guild

Under the Patronage of
Her Majesty Queen Ingrid

The Danish Handcraft Guild was founded in 1928 to promote the spread of interest in needlework and crafts in Denmark. The idea behind the foundation was to preserve old Danish textile traditions while supporting contemporary innovation in the field of embroidery, knitting and other Danish crafts.

From its design office and workshop, artists and craftsmen create designs which are published or produced as kits. The Guild produces a quarterly, bilingual, (Danish/English) magazine which provides information and news for its numerous members in Denmark and abroad. It also publishes embroidery books, one of the most popular of which is a calendar of cross stitch designs contributed by various well-known artists including Her Majesty Queen Margrethe, the Danish Queen.

Materials and instructions

The patterns in this book are worked on 12 B linen or 10 B linen with Danish Flower Thread (Dansk Blomstergarn).

12 B linen, bleached:
Evenweave linen, 30 threads to the inch, 64 inches wide (160 cm). Danish Flower Thread: work with 1 strand using tapestry needle number 24.

10 B linen, bleached:
Evenweave linen, 27 threads to the inch. 60 inches wide (150 cm): Danish Flower Thread: work with 1 strand using tapestry needle number 22.

1 square on pattern = 2×2 threads of linen.
NB: When working petit point: 1 square on pattern = 1×1 thread of linen.

On all the patterns, arrows indicate the center lines. The intersection of these lines is the center of the pattern.

For some of the motifs Cross Stitch Thread (Amagergarn) is used: work with 1 strand. Silk: work with 1 strand, without tightening it.

The linen used in this book is a Danish evenweave called HF Linen which provides an excellent background for the cross stitch embroidery but the same effect can be obtained using a similar evenweave linen. Danish Flower Thread is a fine, matte cotton thread available in over 100 shades (see page 9). All materials are produced by the Danish Handcraft Guild and can be obtained through the stocklists listed on page 64.

Method of working

The patterns in the book are created in cross stitch. The different colors used are shown as symbols and numbers under the pattern diagrams. (In certain patterns back stitch and petit point are also used. The symbols for these are shown on the color keys to the left of the cross stitch symbols).
The illustration on the opposite page shows the range of colors used in Danish Flower Thread with the appropriate numbers adjacent.

Cross stitch
A. Cross stitch from left to right. The underhalf of the stitch is made first, working crosswise over two threads of linen from the lower left-hand corner to the upper right-hand corner. The upper half of the stitch is made backwards as shown.
B. Cross stitch worked up and down. Each stitch is completed in one operation, so that the upper half of the stitch is in the same direction as in A. The wrong side of both A and B appears as vertical rows of stitches.
C. Cross stitches displaced in relation to each other.
D. Four $\frac{3}{4}$ cross stitches are shown on the left. On the right are half cross stitches covering one thread lengthwise and two threads crosswise.

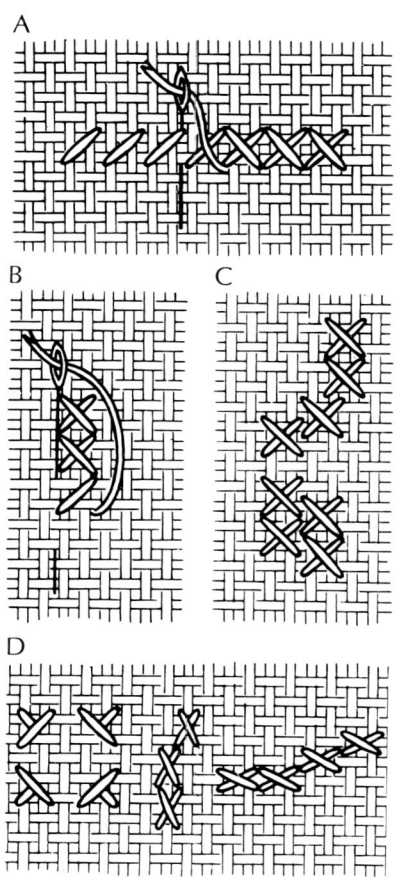

Back stitch
A. In the left-hand illustration the upper stitches are made by inserting the needle two threads to the side and two threads down, one upright stitch passes over two threads and one horizontal stitch over two threads. In the right-hand illustration the upper stitch is made two threads down but only one to the side, and one of the stitches (the fourth), is made two threads to the side and one thread down. In addition one stitch and one horizontal stitch are shown.
B. Four back stitches: two worked over a single thread and two worked on a single intersection.

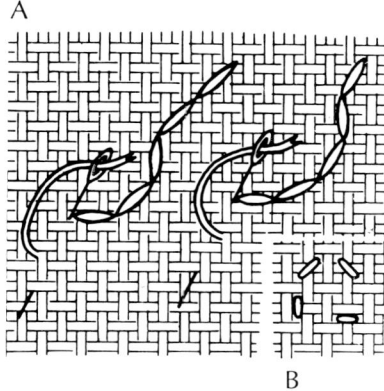

Petit point
Work petit point horizontally from the right to the left, each stitch taken diagonally over one thread.

The color key above indicates which Danish Flower Threads have been used for the embroideries in the book.

Examples of finished work

Runner
12 B linen
Cutting measurements: $12\frac{5}{8} \times 39\frac{3}{8}$ in (32×100 cm).
Finished measurements: $8 \times 35\frac{3}{8}$ in (20×92 cm).
Find center of the shorter edge of the linen.
Measure $2\frac{3}{8}$ in (6 cm) up from the edge and begin the embroidery at arrow.
Distance between the two motifs about $23\frac{1}{2}$ in (60 cm).
Fold the linen 22 threads from the embroidery. Sew a hem 7 threads wide, hem-stitching over 3 threads.

Wall hanging
12 B linen
Cutting measurements: $15\frac{3}{4} \times 15\frac{3}{4}$ in (40×40 cm).
Finished measurements: $10\frac{1}{2} \times 10\frac{1}{2}$ in (27×27 cm).
Find center of the pattern with the help of the arrows.
Find the center of the linen. Begin here.
Mount the finished embroidery on cardboard.

Cushion
10 B linen
Cutting measurements: $14\frac{1}{2} \times 29\frac{1}{2}$ in (37×75 cm).
Finished measurements: $11\frac{1}{2} \times 11\frac{1}{2}$ in (29×29 cm).
Find the center of the pattern with the help of the arrows.
Find the center of the linen. Begin here.
Piece cushion together with piping around edge.

Doily
12 B linen
Cutting measurements: 9×9 in (23×23 cm).
Finished measurements: 6×6 in (15×15 cm).
Find the center of the pattern with the help of the arrows.
Find center of the linen. Begin here.
Sew a hem 7 threads wide, hem-stitching over 3 threads.

Place mat
12 B linen
Cutting measurements: $15\frac{3}{4} \times 21$ in (40×53 cm).
Finished measurements: $11\frac{3}{4} \times 16$ in (30×41 cm).
Measure $2\frac{1}{4}$ in (6 cm) in and down from the top lefthand corner. Begin the border here. Fold under the linen 7 threads from the embroidery and sew a hem 7 threads wide.

In addition to the suggestions on the opposite page the photograph shows how you can apply your designs to a variety of pretty articles.

11

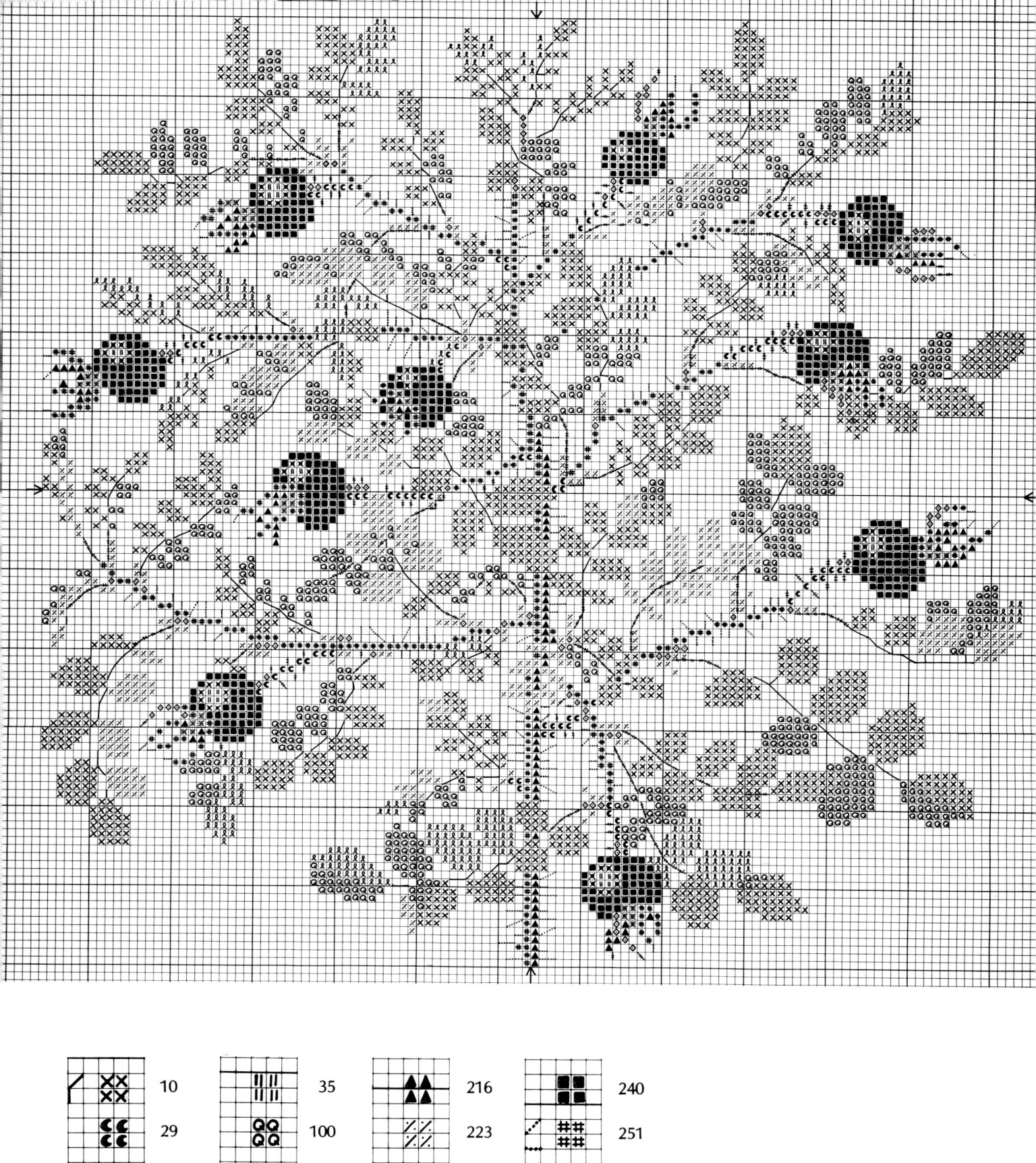

ROSA PIMPINELLIFOLIA

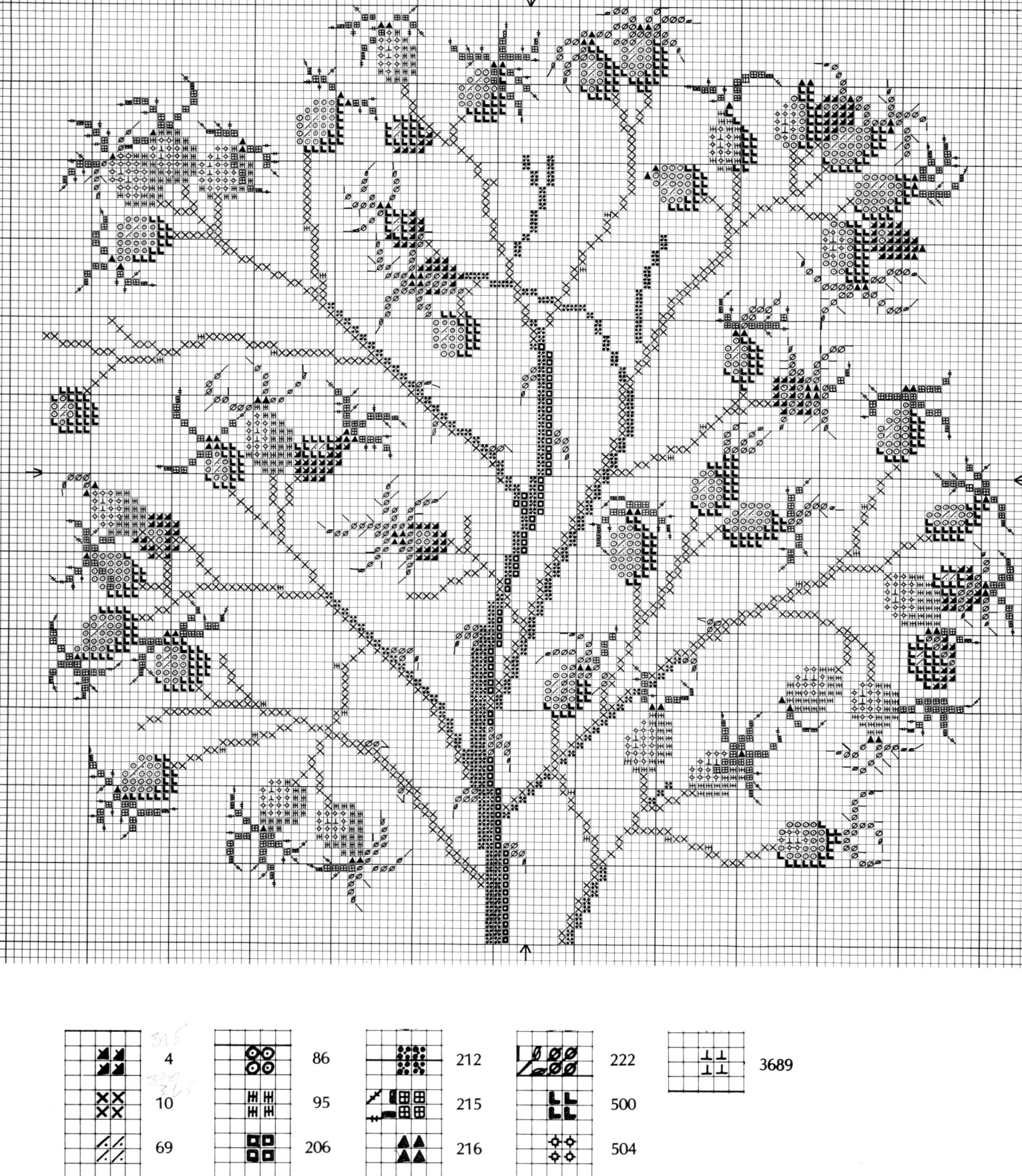

Eglantine – Sweet Briar

ROSA RUBIGINOSA

Field Rose

ROSA ARVENSIS

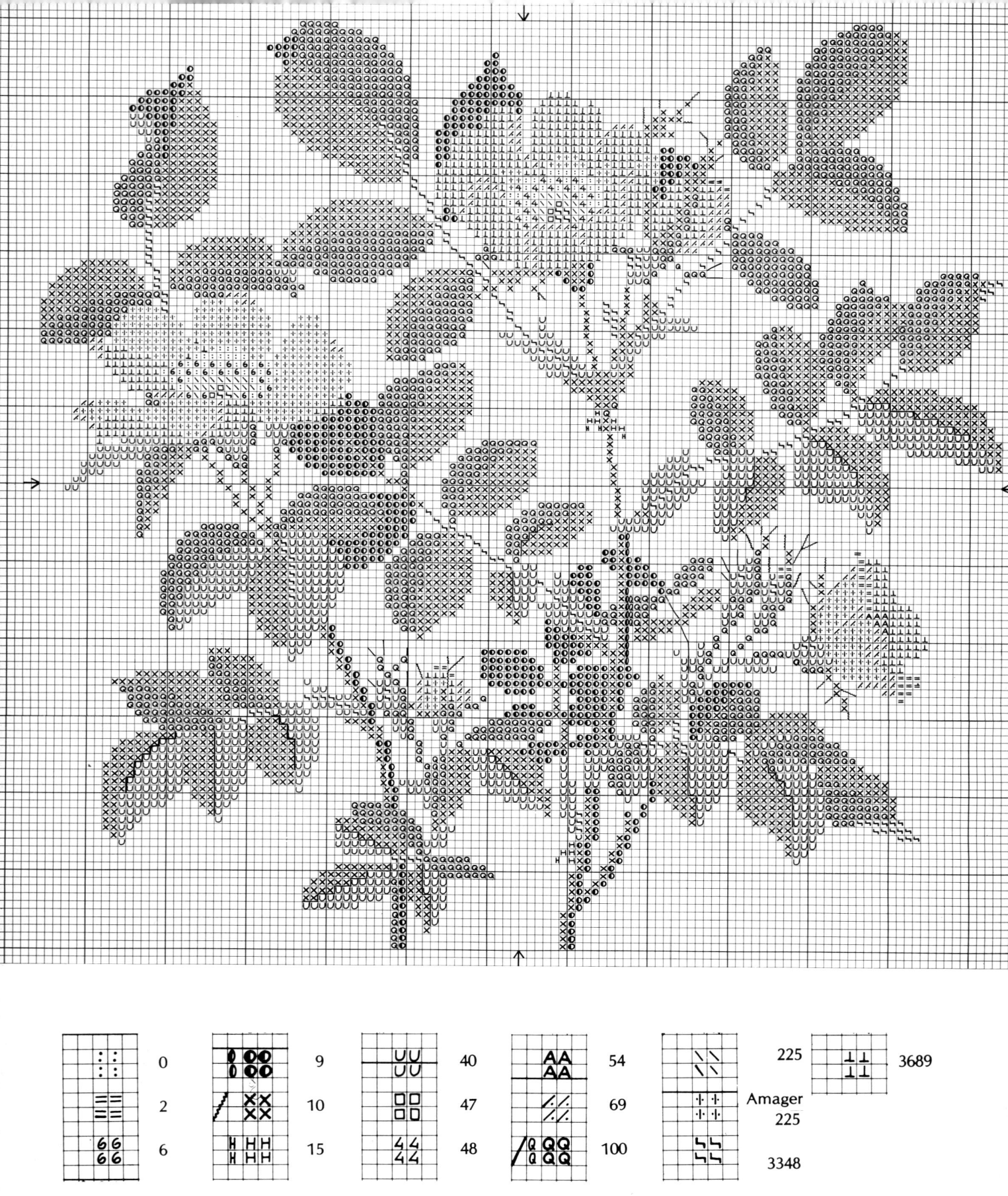

Dog Rose

ROSA CANINA

ROSA VIRGINIANA

120 H x 120 W

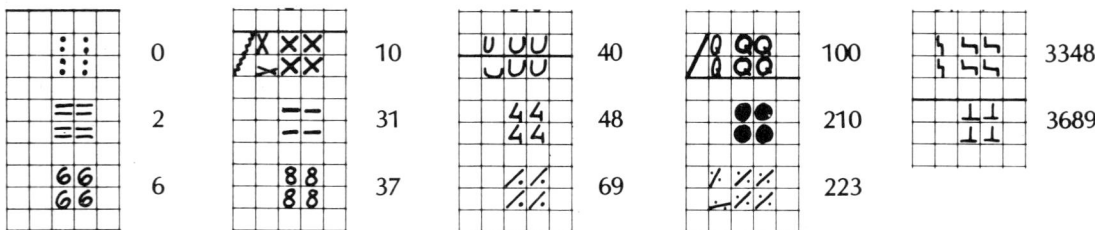

	0		10		40		100		3348
	2		31		48		210		3689
	6		37		69		223		

Eglantine – Sweet Briar

ROSA RUBIGINOSA

120H x 120W

XX	10	QQ	100	╱╱	223	11 505
UU	40	◊◊	205	╲╲	225	mm 602
44	48	●●	210	✳✳	411	ZZ 603

ROSA RUGOSA

120 H x 120 W

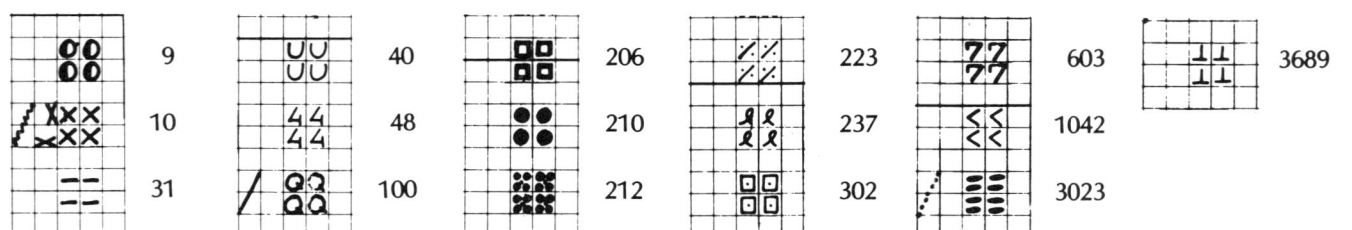

9	40	206	223	603	3689	
10	48	210	237	1042		
31	100	212	302	3023		

French Rose

ROSA GALLICA

'Nevada'

ROSA MOYESII

10
86
210
215
222
223
238
302
323
411
500
504
506
3348
3689

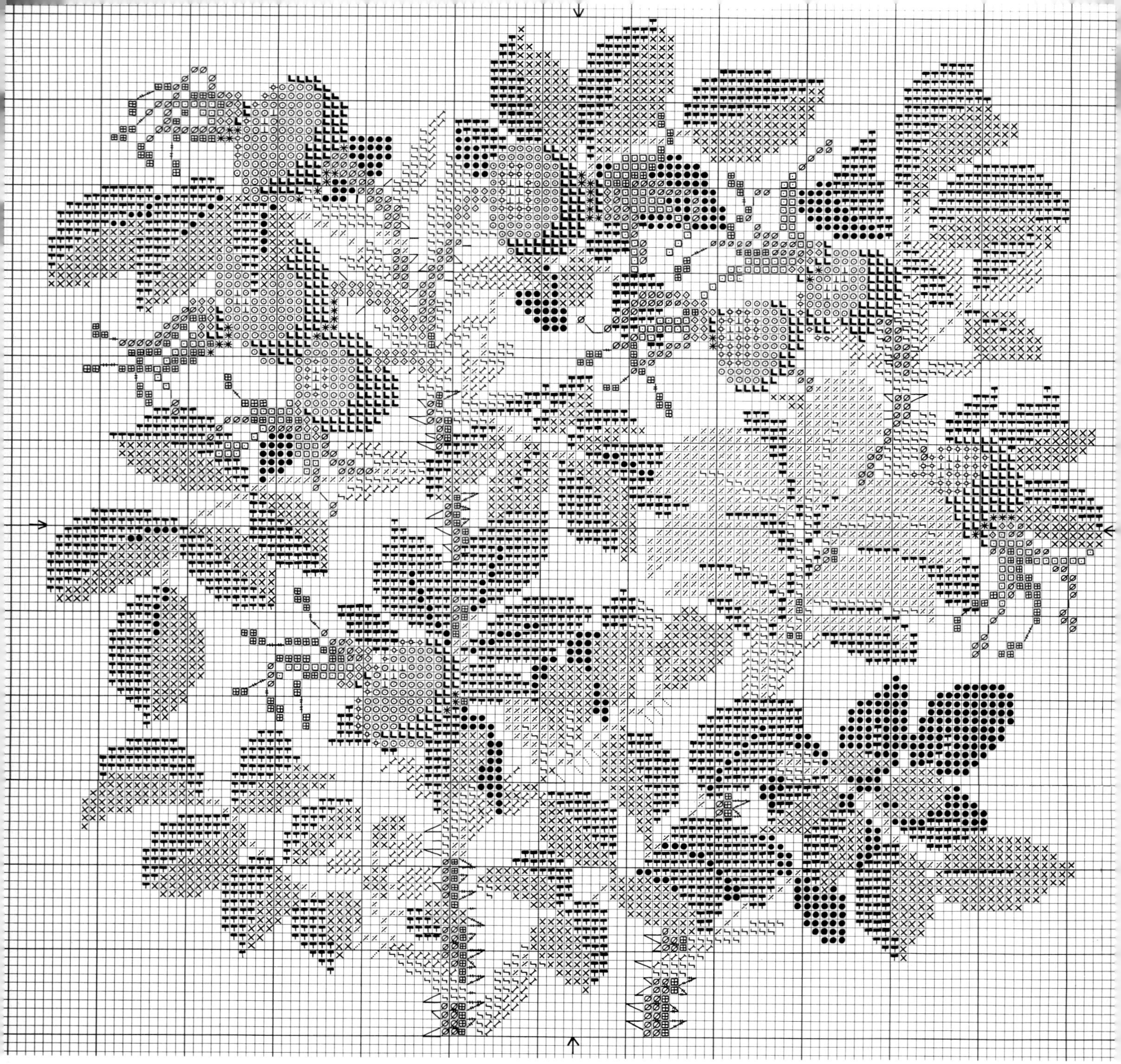

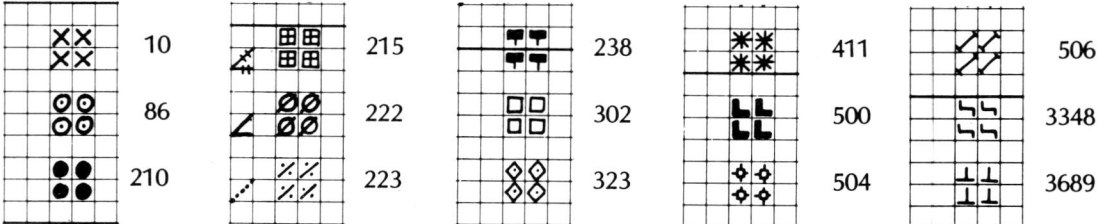

'Frau Dagmar Hartopp'

ROSA RUGOSA

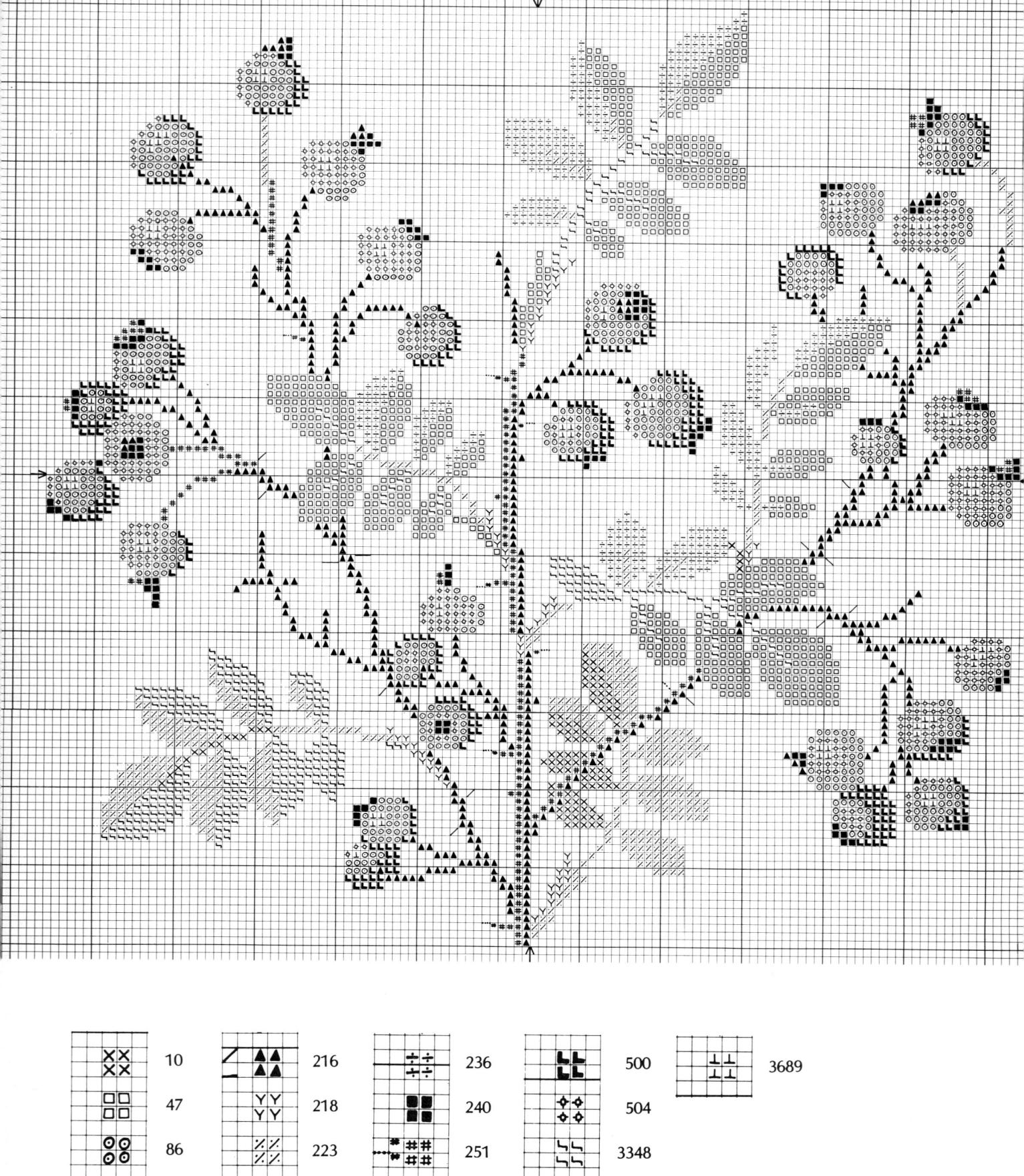

ROSA NITIDA

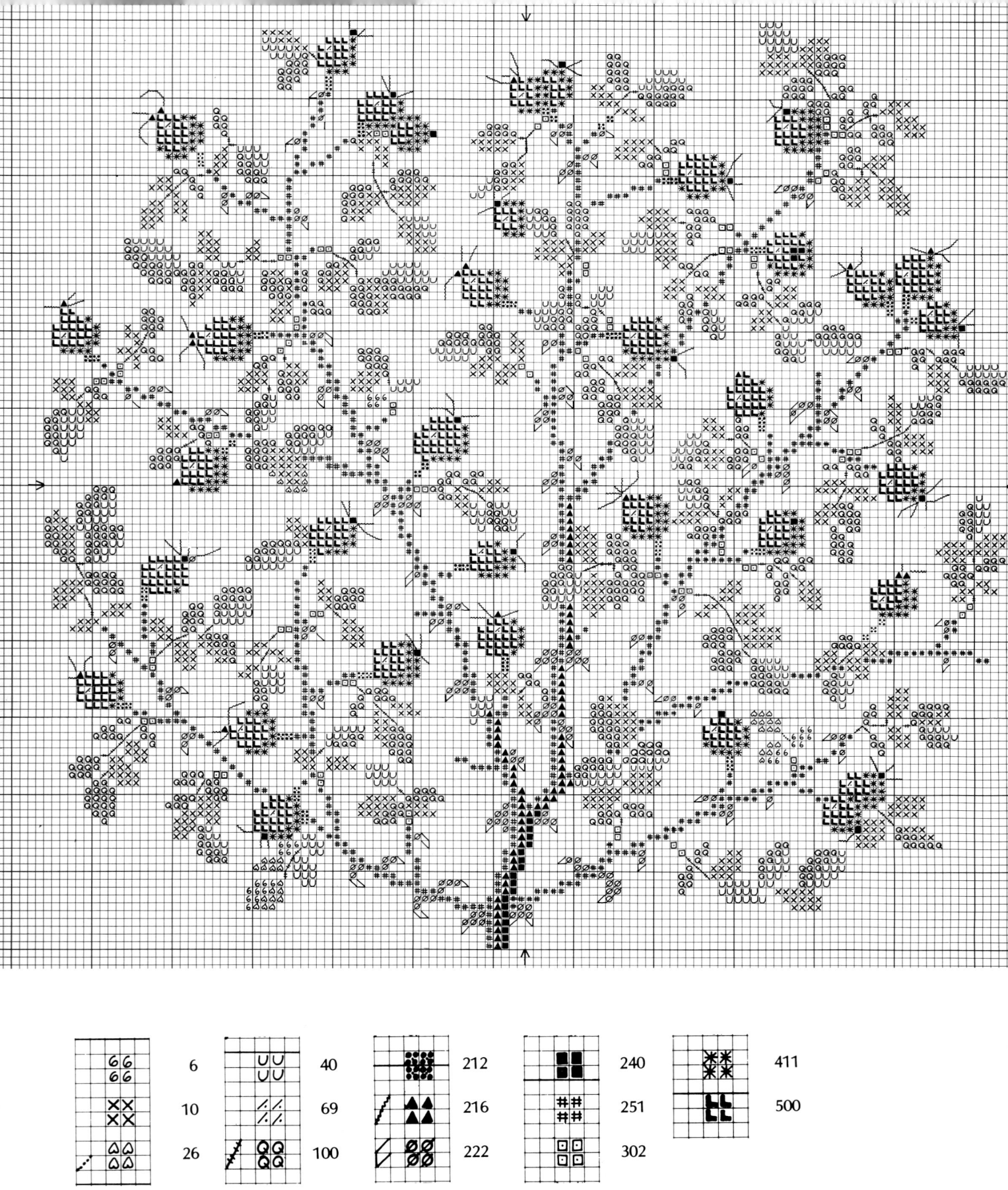

ROSA SERAFINE

9
10
15
37
40
88
100
205
216
223
236
250
251
323
411
506

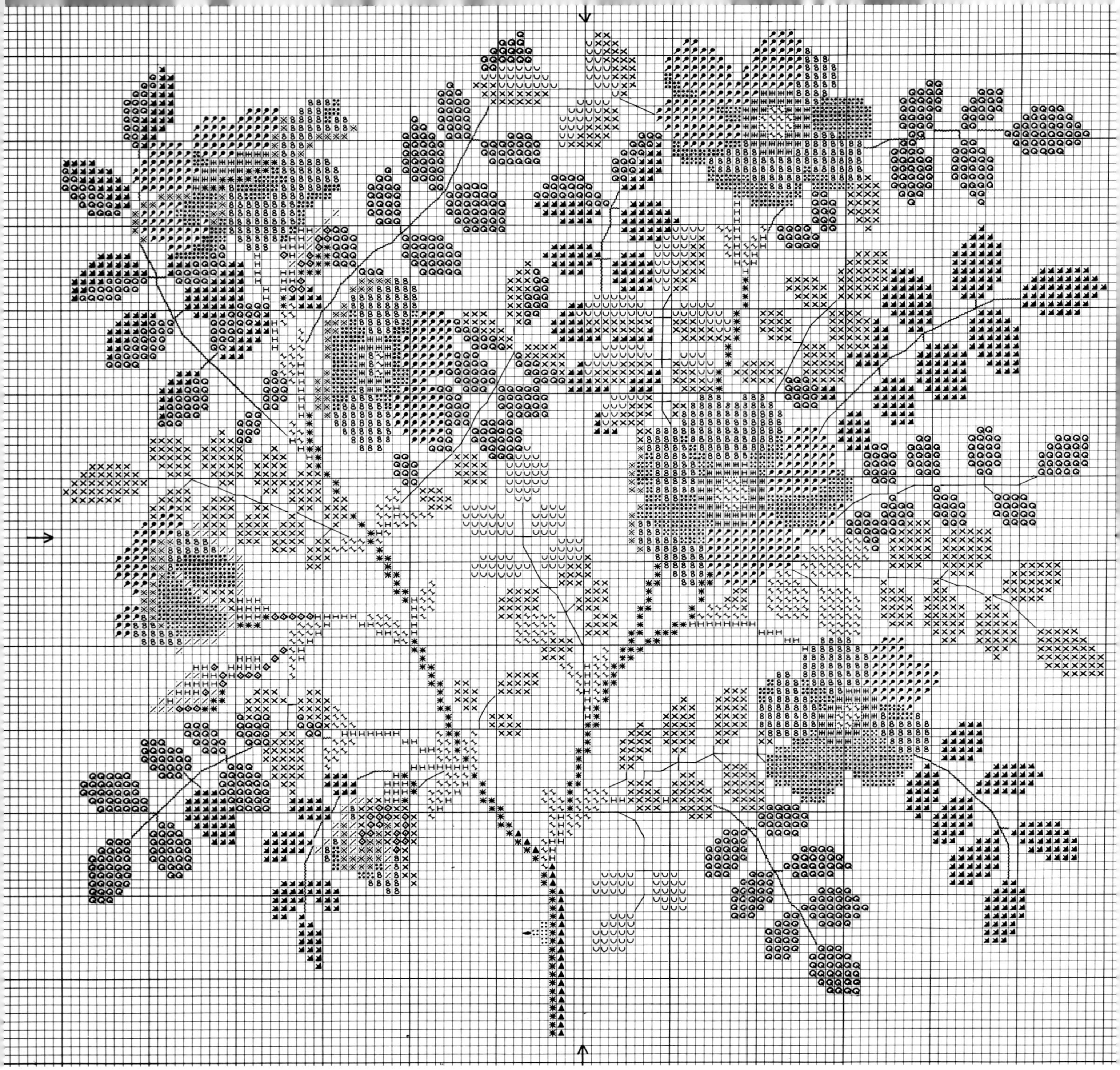

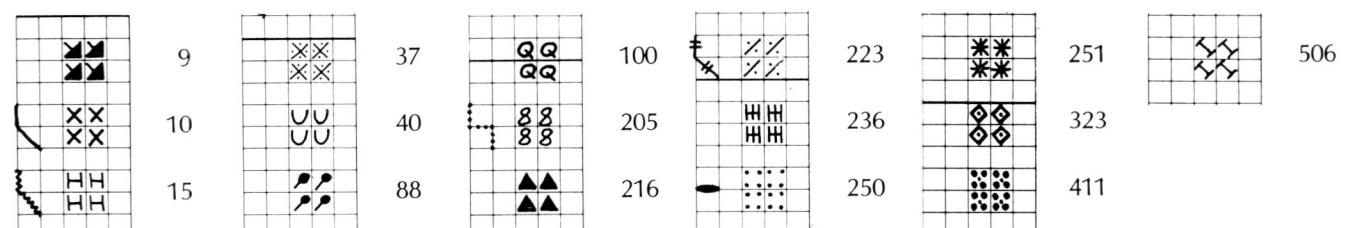

ROSA MOYESII

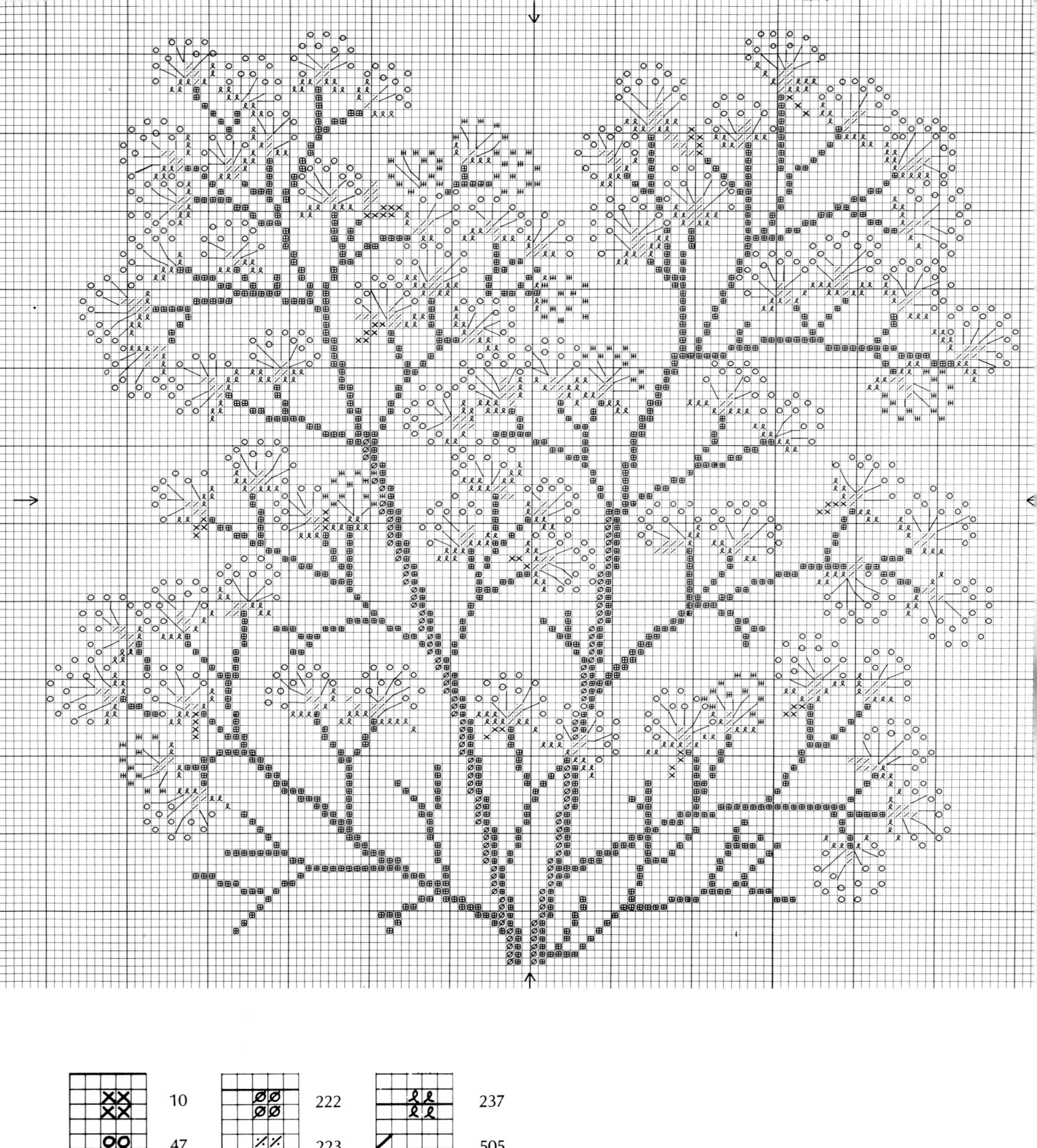

Cornelian Cherry

CORNUS MAS

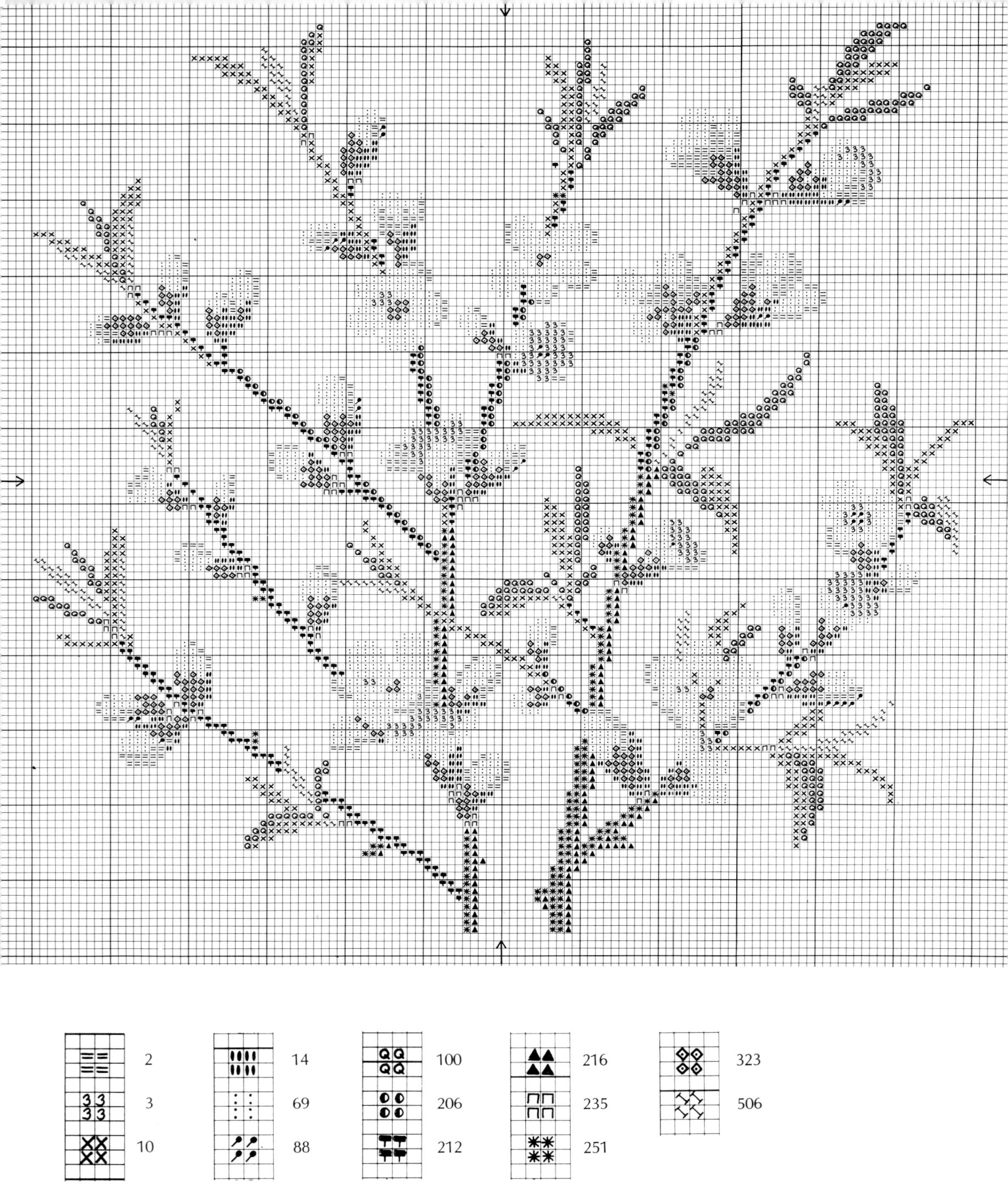

Ornamental Almond

PRUNUS PERSICA

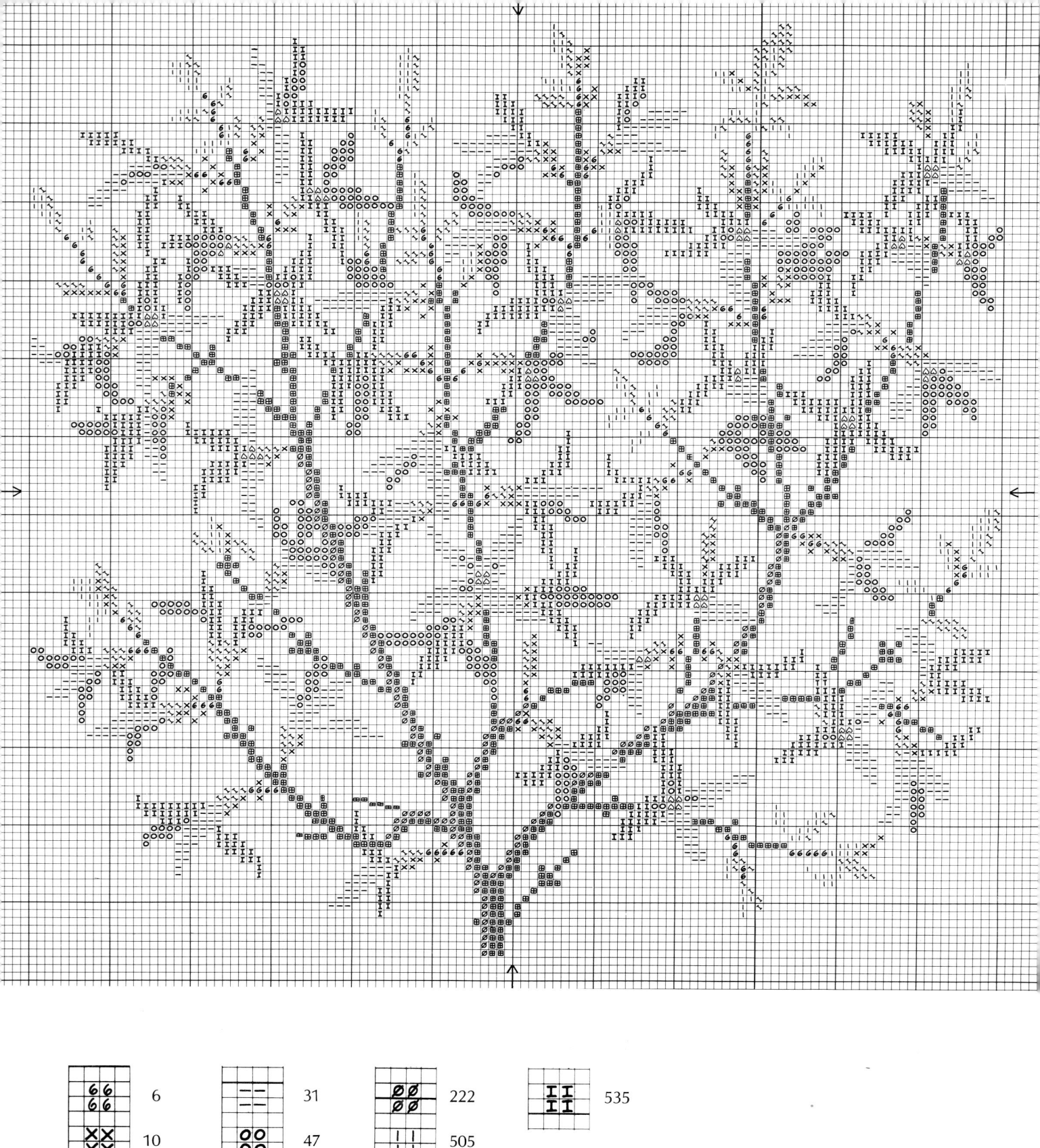

Symbol	Code
6	6
×	10
△	26
−	31
○	47
⊞	215
∅	222
│	505
↘	506
I	535

Forsythia

FORSYTHIA INTERMEDIA

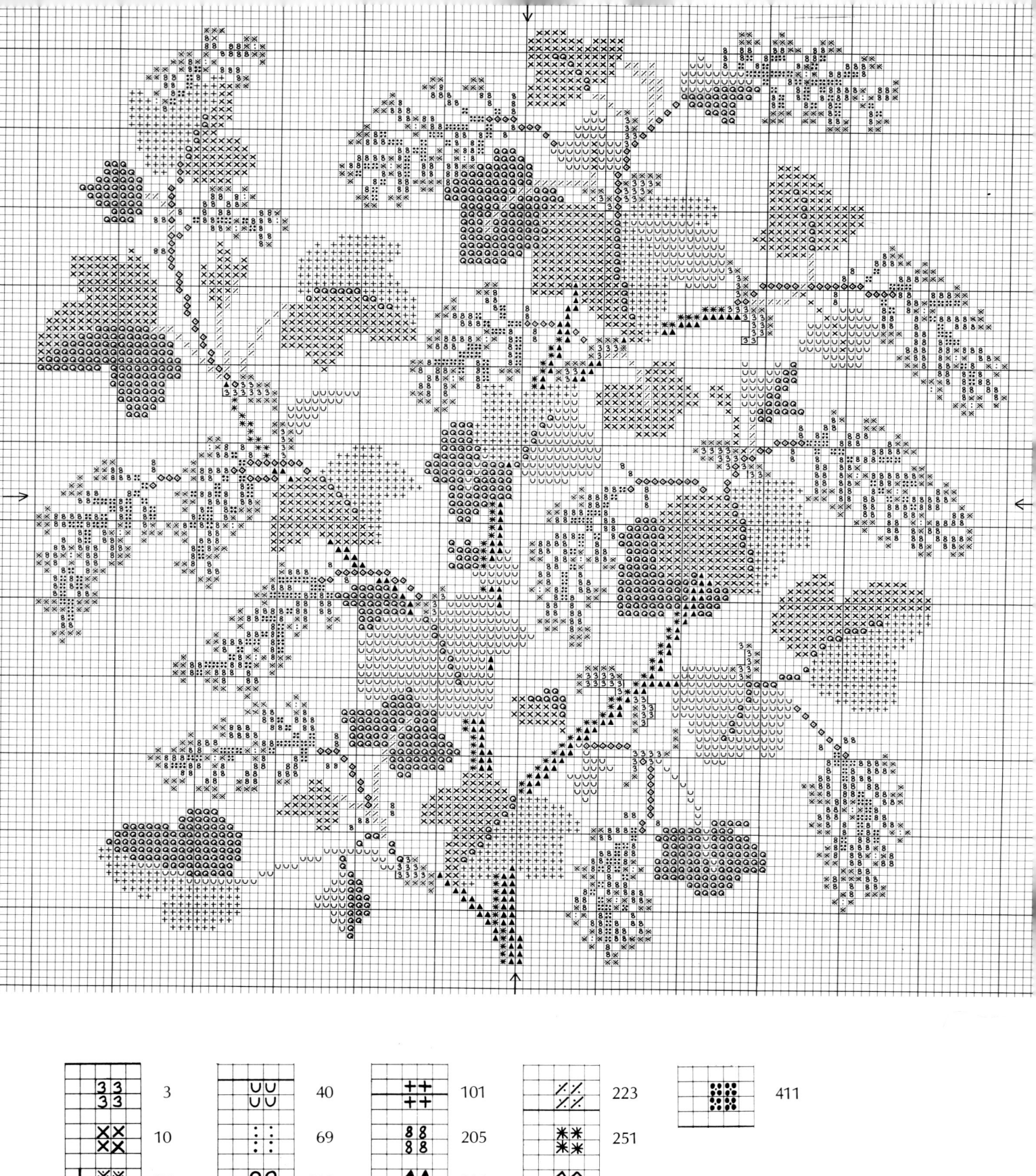

Flowering Currant

RIBES SANGUINEUM

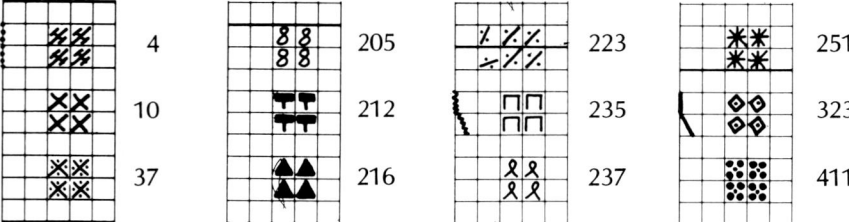

	4		205		223	251
	10		212		235	323
	37		216		237	411

Crab Apple

MALUS PURPUREA

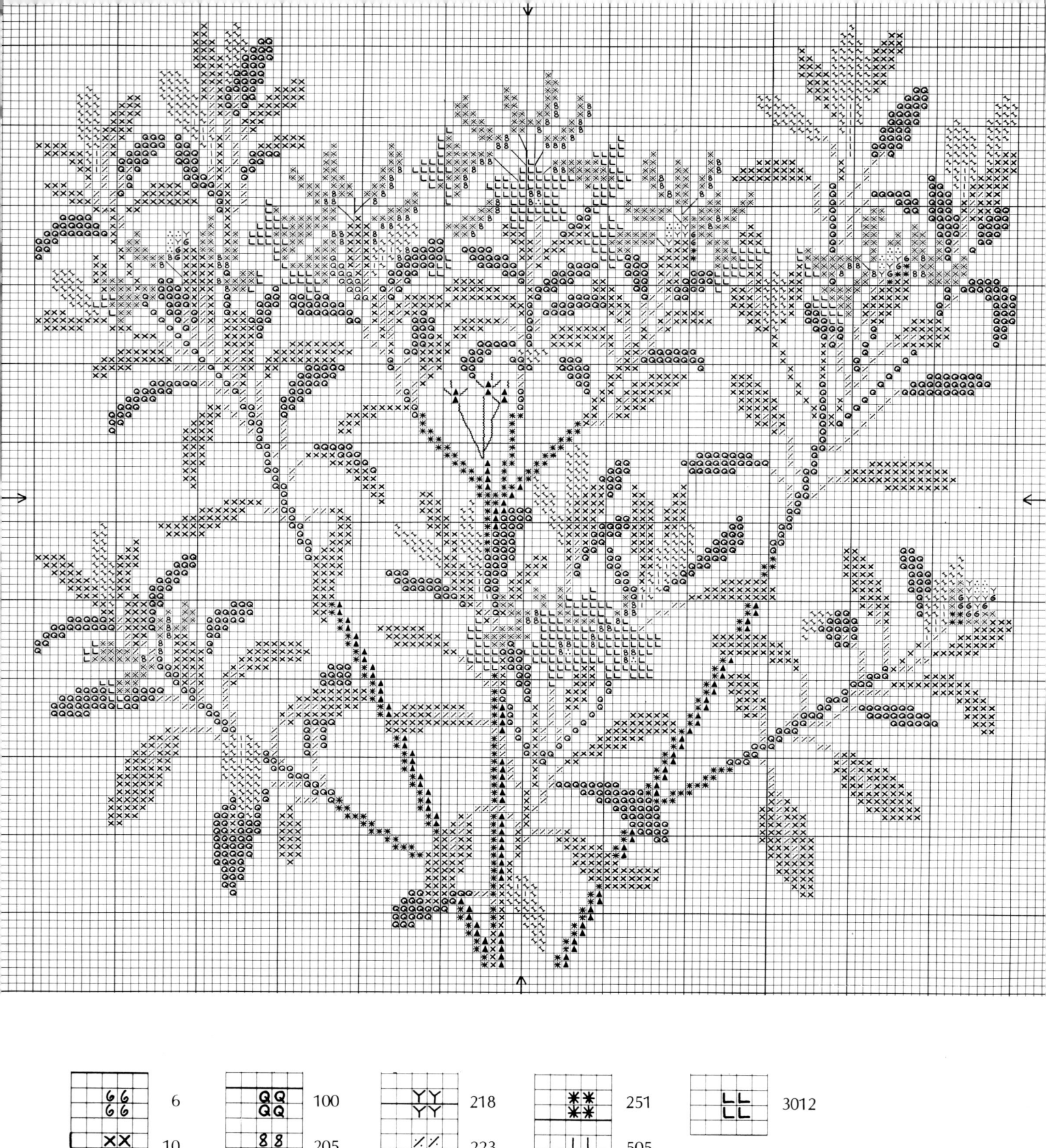

RHODODENDRON HIRSUTUM

2
10
37
69
100
210
215
223
302
323
506
1012

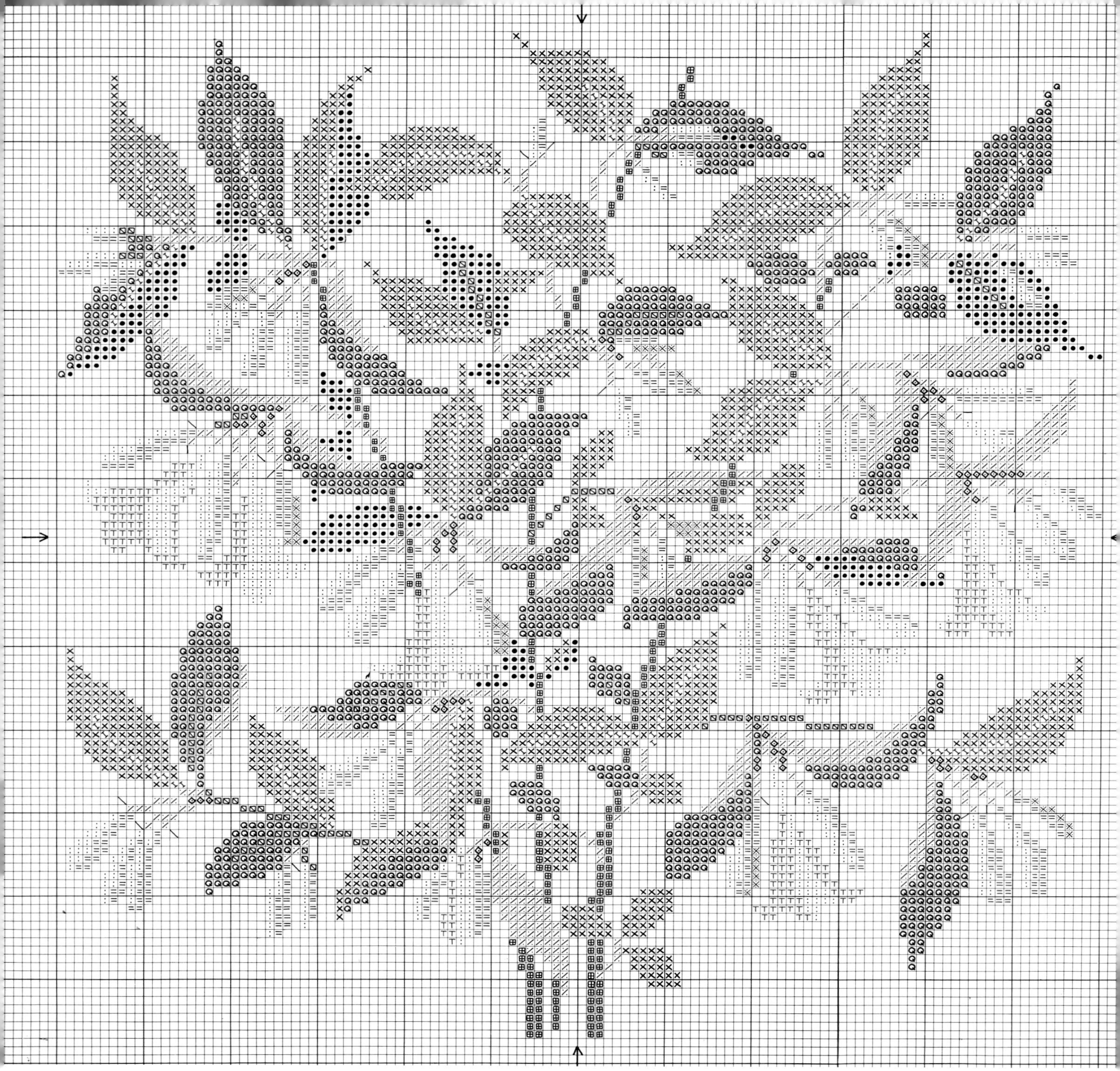

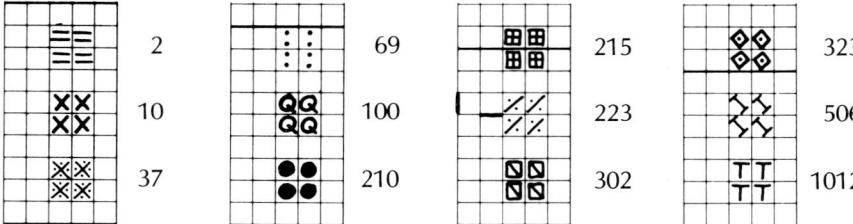

WEIGELA FLORIDA

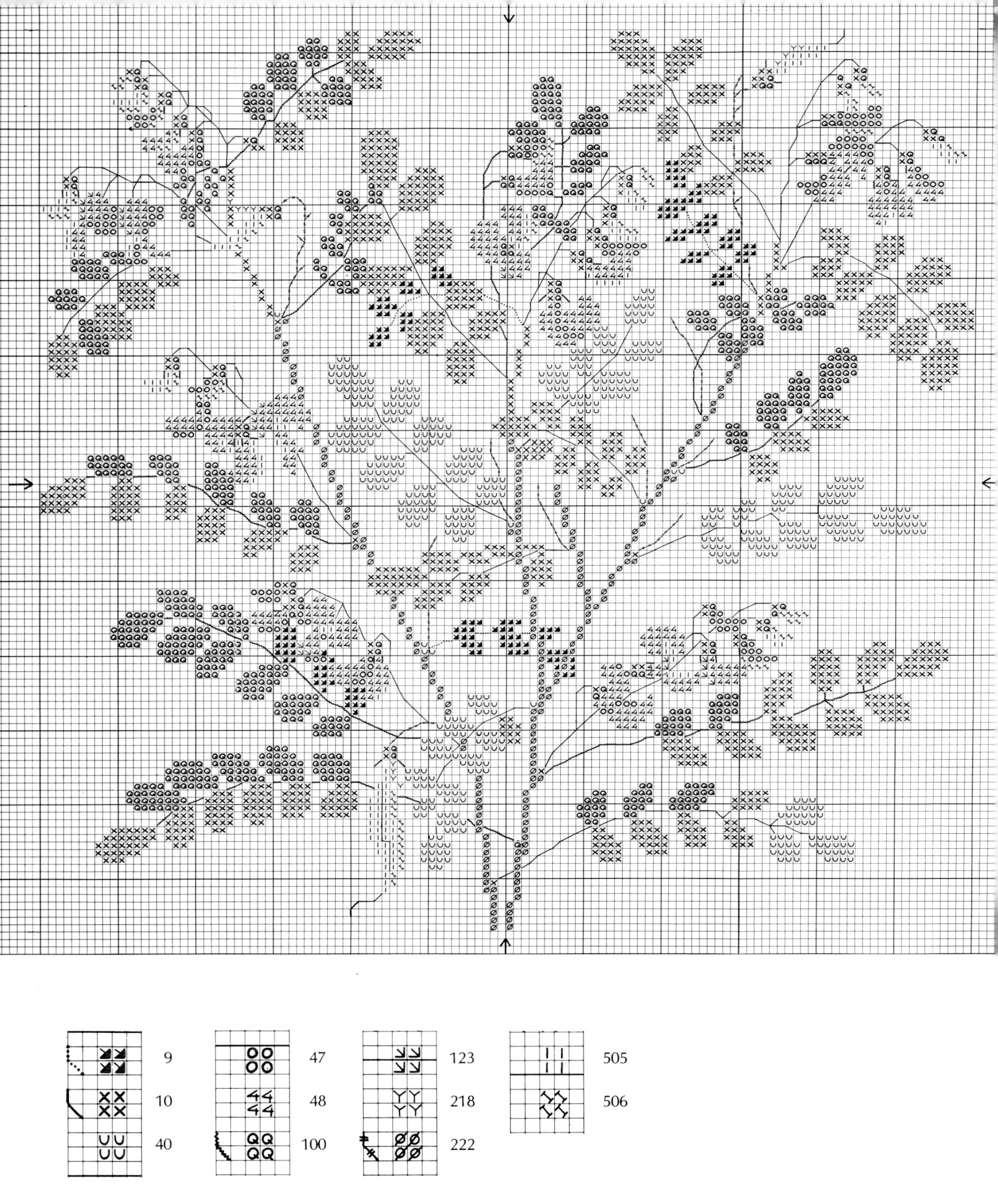

Senna

COLUTEA ARBORESCENS

Japanese Quince

CHAENOMELES LAGENARIA

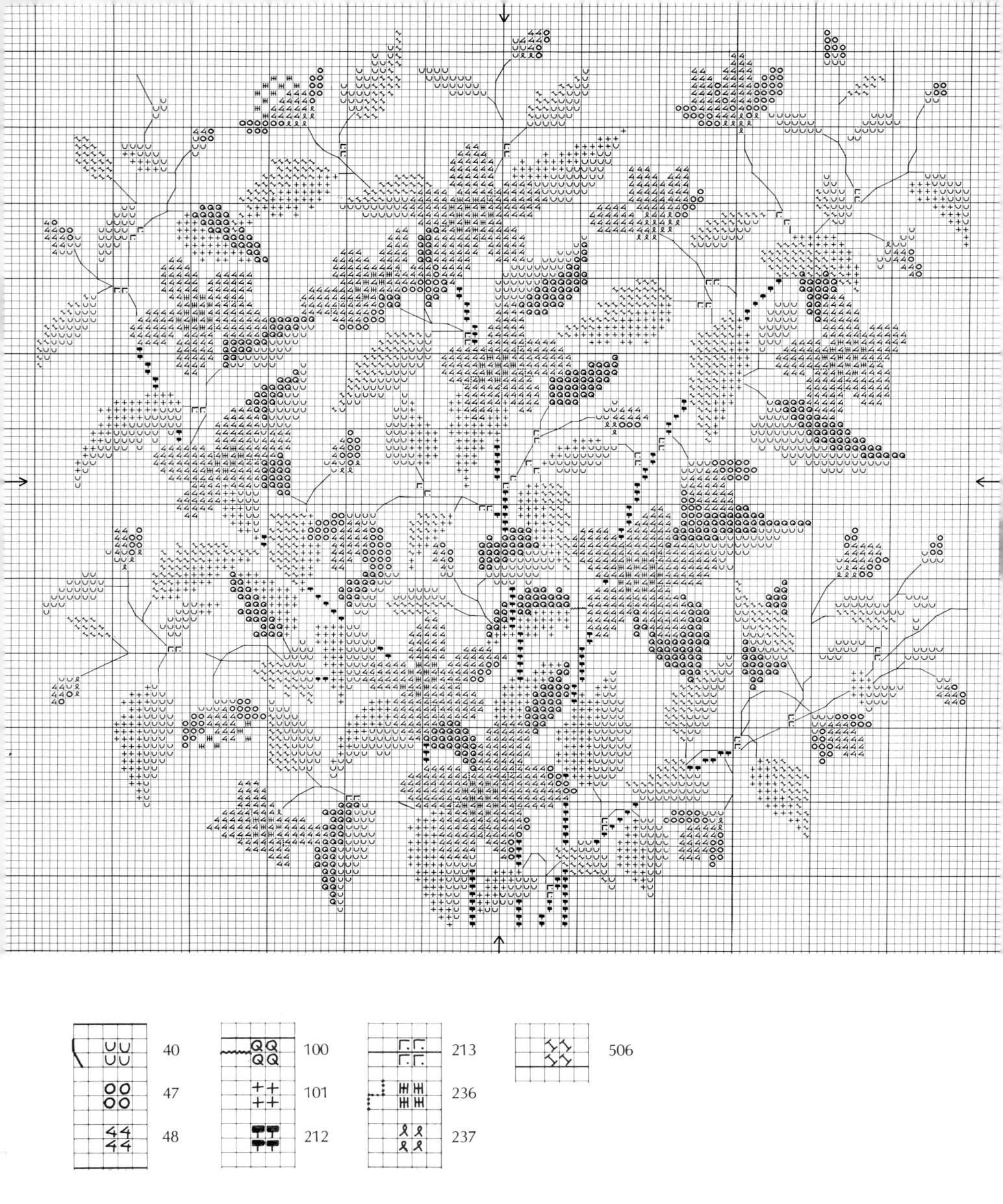

KERRIA JAPONICA

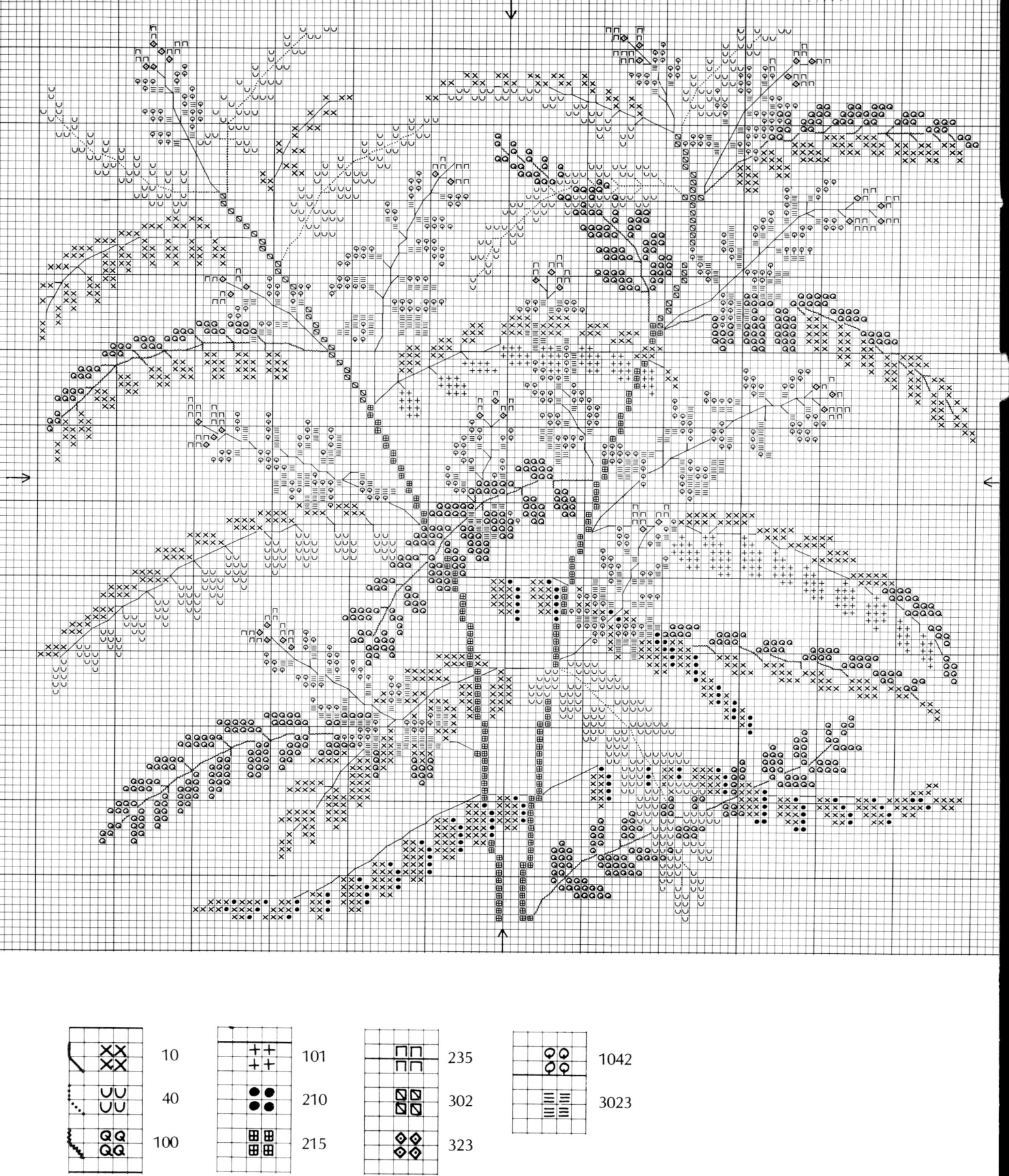

INDIGOFERA GERARDIANA

2
4
9
10
29
37
48
100
205
210
216
218
223
225
323

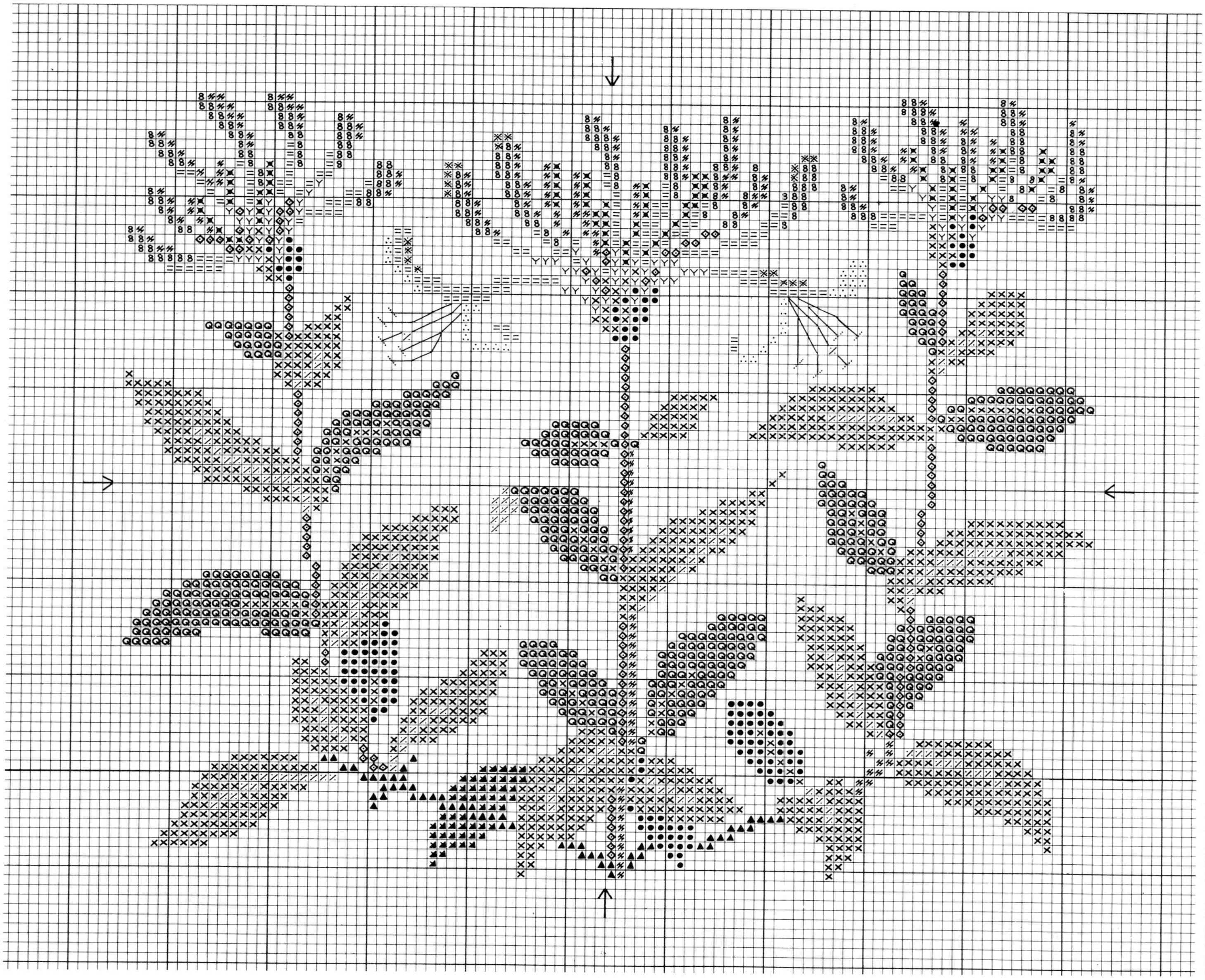

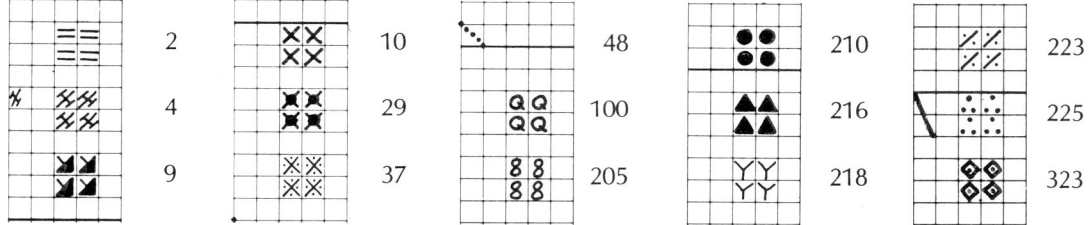

Honeysuckle

LONICERA PERICLYMENUM

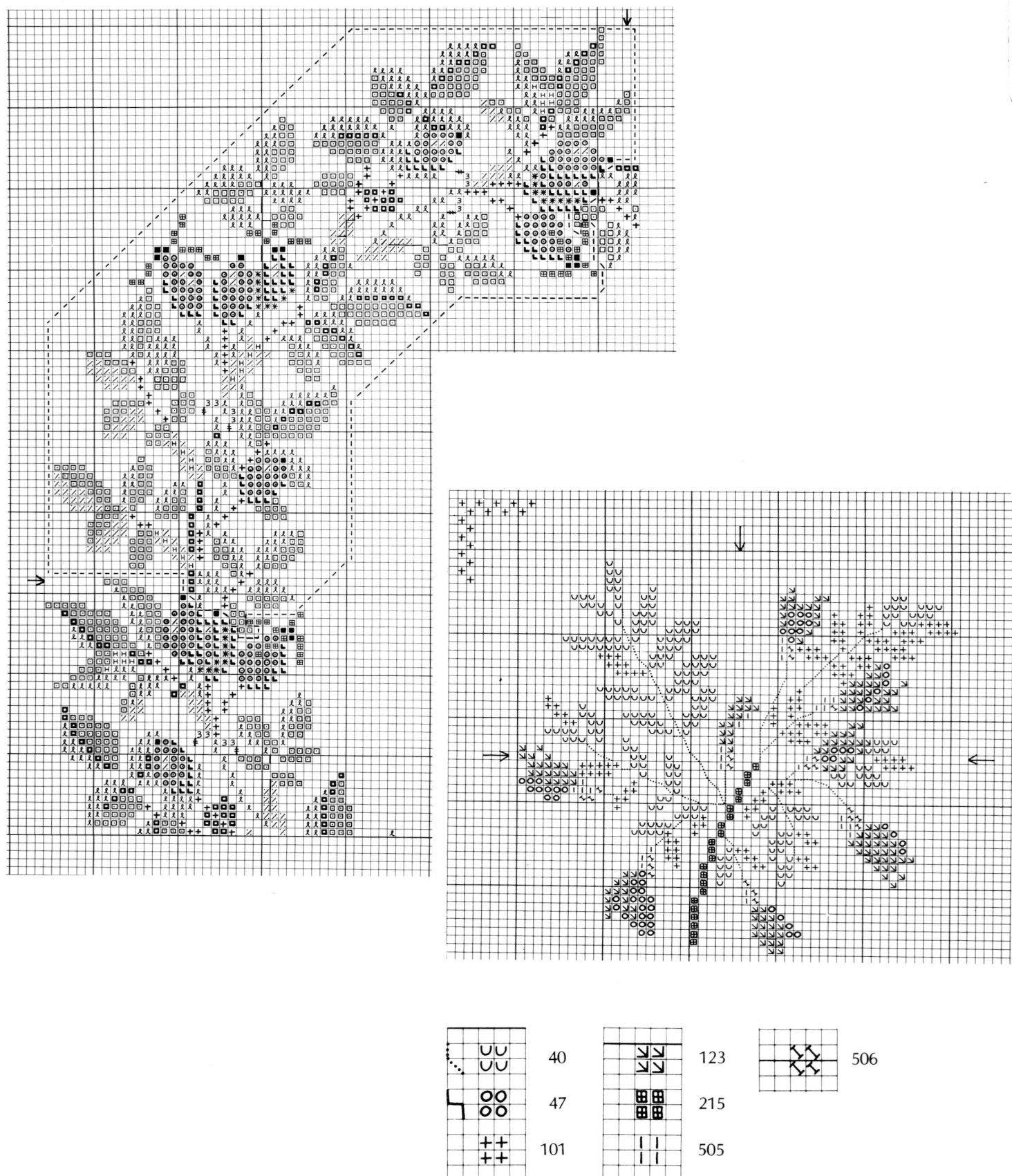

Dog Rose

ROSA CANINA

CARAGANA FRUCTICOSA

List of patterns

2 *Rosa virginiana* (see illustration on cover).
13 *Rosa pimpinellifolia*
15 *Rosa rubiginosa* (Eglantine – Sweet Briar)
17 *Rosa Arvensis* (Field Rose)
19 *Rosa canina* (Dog Rose)
21 *Rosa virginiana*
23 *Rosa rubiginosa* (Eglantine – Sweet Briar)
25 *Rosa rugosa*
27 *Rosa gallica* (French Rose)
29 *Rosa moyesii* ('Nevada')
31 *Rosa rugosa* ('Frau Dagmar Hartopp')
33 *Rosa nitida*
35 *Rosa serafine*
37 *Rosa moyesii*
39 *Comus mas* (Cornelian Cherry)
41 *Prunus persica* (Ornamental Almond)
43 *Forsythia intermedia*
45 *Ribes sanguineum* (Flowering currant)
47 *Malus purpurea* (Crab apple)
49 *Rhododendron hirsutum*
51 *Wiegela florida*
53 *Colutea arborescens* (Senna)
55 *Chaenomeles lagenaria* (Japanese Quince)
57 *Kerria japonica*
59 *Indigofera gerardiana*
61 *Lonicera periclymenum* (Honeysuckle)
63 *Caragana fructicosa and Rosa canina* (Dog Rose)

Suppliers in the United States

The following U.S. suppliers will be happy to give you information about Danish Flower Threads as well as other threads and linen:

American Crewel and Canvas Studio
P. O. Box 453
Canastota NY 13032

The Counting House
P. O. Box 155
Pawley's Island SC 29585

Needle Art Studio
17700 West Capitol Drive
Brookfield WI 53005

The Strawberry Studio
7 Olde Ridge Village
Chaddsford PA 19317